ROCK AND WATER GARDENS

Dwarf tulips planted in a rock
garden bordering a pool

**YOUR GARDEN
IN COLOUR
SERIES**

ROCK AND
WATER GARDENS

Compiled and edited by
Ron Brown

WARD LOCK LIMITED · LONDON

SBN 7063 1499 9

Ward Lock Limited, 116 Baker Street,
London W1M 2BB

Impreso en los Talleres de EDITORIAL FHER, S. A.
Calle Villabaso, 9.– BILBAO-ESPAÑA

PRINTED IN SPAIN

There are few features in the garden that provide such a variety of interests in so little space as a well-planned and carefully planted rock garden. The smallest plot may contain a rock garden which will house a representative and charming collection of alpine plants; but, on the other hand, there are few features in the ordinary garden that are so neglected and so ill-understood. It must be remembered that the chief function of the rock garden is to provide the plants grown in it with conditions, so far as possible, similar to those existing in their natural haunts.

The alpines and high alpines are the most typical of all rock plants and are mostly natives of the high mountain crags and screes of the Alps and Himalayas. The ideal rock garden, therefore, should, so far as possible, provide the soil and natural conditions pertaining in these regions. During the short alpine summer the plants are subjected to fierce and baking sun; many of them, therefore, have thick leaves covered with down or hair to protect them from its shrivelling rays. The roots, too, at this time need ample moisture, and this is provided by the melting of the snows on the mountain tops, whence it permeates through the scree of the moraine; it will also be seen that to live in their natural haunts they require to be very deep and strong rooted, very often with a much greater root run than the foliage and flowers which their roots support. In winter, this downy foliage, which rots very rapidly if there is excessive moisture overhead or round the crowns of the plants, is protected by a blanket of snow until spring and summer again come round. It is obvious, therefore, that the two essential requirements of alpine plants, especially high alpines, are ample cool drainage for the soil in which they grow, where their roots can penetrate to a good depth, and protection from damp in winter. The former can be obtained with a little care during the construction of the rock garden, and the latter essential can be provided by the use of panes of glass and hand-lights placed over these downy-leaved plants (it is not necessary with glossy-leaved species) in winter. It is against damp and the atmospheric pollution of many low-lying areas, not frost, that these plants need most protection.

Rock cress (Ababis)

Thrift or Sea Pink ((Armeria)

6

A rock garden of this type can be scaled
up or down to suit the size of garden

Small outcrops of rock placed as shown here
can greatly enhance a garden, especially on a sloping site

Rocks and stones

As already mentioned, most of the alpines have to withstand considerable drought during the short, but parching, summer months. For this reason, and because there is often but scanty surface soil, the majority of them have long, running roots that can penetrate deeply into crevices among the rocks and thus draw moisture and nourishment from below. Deep crevices, packed with a rich, well-drained mixture of soil suitable to the plants, are, therefore, of primary importance in the rock garden.

The horrible mass of shiny, glazed lumps of brickwork in the cracks of which half-starved ferns and plants struggle for existence is nothing but a disfigurement.

The chief uses of the rocks and stones in a rock garden are the provision of coolness for the roots and the provision of moisture in crevices for the use of the plants when required, and this is not in winter when water would rot the plants and not grow them. But the idea that rock plants grow best in practically nothing but rock is a mistaken one. As pointed out before, a generous allowance of good soil between, amongst, and beneath the stones is essential for the healthy growth of the plants. As the function of the rocks is to provide shelter for roots, it is clearly useless to plant slabs of rock or stone perpendicularly in the soil unless by so doing the stones are very close together and tightly packed where possible with the mixture as previously mentioned. The stones should not be planted like monuments in a cemetery. The roots must get down beneath them, or otherwise they do not preserve any moisture.

For the beginner, the easiest way is to use large masses of stones, two or more feet in length and six to twenty-four inches in depth, where possible, and they should be sunk well and firmly in the earth in a slightly slanting direction—tilted backwards, not forwards, so that the rain may trickle down to the roots of the plants and quickly get away.

If the rocks lean forward, over the plants, the roots will be sheltered from the rain and probably parched. Although the visible portions of the rocks in the garden should be as pleasing as may be to the eye, and should all slant in the same direction to represent a natural outcrop or stratum of stone, it should never be forgotten that they are not there for the sake of picturesque effect only, but to protect the roots of the plants growing among them.

The slopes of the mounds in which the boulders are set must be as natural in appearance as possible; there should be miniature ranges and mountain peaks and, dividing them, valleys into which spurs from the hills project. Winding paths, eighteen inches to two feet in width, with stepping-stones, should be cut through these gorges so that every part of the rock garden may be easily accessible. The pockets in which the alpines are to be planted should be irregular in shape and may vary from a few inches in diameter to as many feet across. Their surfaces must not be flat, but sloping to afford drainage. They must provide ample root-run and should be from a foot to eighteen inches in depth, and so constructed that the soil will not wash out of them. If there is any chance of the soil in the pockets becoming sodden, six to twelve inches of clinker and rubble drainage must be provided to offset this.

A word about grass

One final suggestion for the real lover of beauty is to pay a visit to one of the more rocky slopes of our national parks, and where the garden is large enough he should endeavour to complete the picture with the aid of the lawn running up or down between the knolls of outcropping stone. When in the heart of some of our more smoky cities only use the indigenous grasses of the area, don't sow seed used for the hayfield, or the garden lover will find that he spends most of his time cutting grass in summer to lose it completely in the frosty fogs of the winter months. The seed of the dwarf-growing grasses is more exclusive and effective, about one to one-and-a-half ounces to the square yard is required, and the money spent is fully repaid. I find a pinch of dwarf wild white clover seed to the pound is often a great help in establishing the turf; better still, select some turf from the immediate neighbourhood and lay it over the surface, then remove the coarser weeds, for whilst one does not require a bowling green surface, the evenness of the surface is of considerable aid when the time comes to mow the area. A covering of pit or sea sand on one or two occasions, brushed in, will gradually secure this surface, if this is not sufficient room to use a small garden roller effectively. One may lay turf throughout the milder periods of our autumn and winter months and sow the seed from March–May or in September.

There are, of course, a number of proprietary articles on the market for removing dicotyledonous weeds; I advise the reader to follow the prescriptions fully when daisies, clover or any other weeds become a nuisance; some of these weed-killers are dangerous, so care should be taken.

I find the construction of the rock garden equal in interest to the painting of a picture to the artist.

Columbine (Aquilegia)

Two varieties of crocuses

An attractive rock garden
in front of a period-st e
house, note the use of shrubs

Soil and situation

Soil

The great mass of rock plants, particularly the alpines, like a rich soil, even where they need little of it. It should, above all, be well drained so as to be light and porous in winter, but at the same time it must be moist and cool in summer. A soil full of coarse sand or grit, leaf-mould, and other decayed vegetable matter, mixed in some cases with old spent manure from a hotbed, is excellent for rock gardening. As a whole these plants are not faddy as to soil and most thrive well in the compost mentioned above, but some grow best in certain soils.

For those requiring special soil conditions it is quite easy to scoop out a hollow and to substitute a little special compost.

Alpine plants in their native habitat receive a yearly top-dressing of vegetable matter from the material carried down by the melting snows, and alpines in a rock garden are all the better for a top-dressing artificially applied in imitation of this natural process.

Where rock plants are studied in their natural conditions, it will be found that in most cases the soil around the roots is completely covered by the stalks and leaves, each plant touching its neighbours, and that practically no soil is left exposed. This arrangement is of the greatest use to the plants, as by preventing the exposure of the soil to the action of sun and wind, its natural moisture is preserved, so that, so far as we can, we should provide this protection. This is, however, rather difficult to do at first, as while the plants are still small and most need protection, they are unable to cover the surface of the ground, and to plant them closer together would merely mean starving and over-crowding them. In such a case the best thing to do is to cover the immediate surface of the soil with chips of stone, small enough to be easily pushed aside by a shoot, but sufficient to prevent the over-drying of the earth.

In a suitable soil and situation the plants should soon spread and clothe the entire surface.

Situation

As regards the situation of the rock garden, it should, where possible, have an open, sunny position, away from walls and trees. The latter will prevent the circulation of fresh air so necessary to alpine plants and, in addition, the roots will soon find their way into the soil provided for the rock plants, and rob it of its nourishment. The rock garden always looks best where it has not to bear contrast with any formal arrangement of garden or shrubbery; a wild and "natural-looking" site, and, where possible, one where the natural rock of the district crops up here and there, is the most favourable.

Suitable stone

In making the garden the stone of the district should always be used where possible, although it is advisable in the dry districts to use a porous sandstone, as this provides a kindlier home for the roots and a cooler stone for the foliage in the long sunny days. The more rugged limestone has a most natural weather-worn appearance and the cracks and crevices provide a cool root-run for the plants in the wetter areas of the north and west coasts. In the industrial areas where there is considerable atmospheric pollution the natural lichen and mosses are quickly removed, leaving a somewhat grim appearance to what should have been a very harmonious picture. The stone chosen should be porous so as to be able to absorb ample moisture: hard, impermeable rocks, like granite, should, therefore, be avoided unless arranged with skill, except in the wetter regions. Any natural rock formation should be used as a basis, the garden being constructed round and among it, the knolls or banks required being built up, not on heaps of stones, but on good soil, with big stones set in out-cropping groups here and there, the surface being set fairly thickly with stones of varying sizes, but all of the same kind. Let the stones be rugged and as massive as the size of the rock garden and one's means will warrant. Here and there set in larger stones, sometimes touching and forming ledges and knolls so that, when these are filled with plants, they give the whole the appearance of solidarity and the bold outlines of natural stratification. It is essential that there shall be no spaces and dry hollows amongst and around the stones, and that the earth shall be well bedded round them.

The paths

The paths through and near the rock garden should not be too formal and their edges should blend softly with the surrounding vegetation. This may be done by making the path of flat rocks or broken paving-stones set in good soil, with small plants at the edges placed actually between the stones, and encouraged to spread over all those parts of the path not habitually walked upon. Even upon the edges of gravel walks this softening process may very well be carried out, if suitable plants are chosen. The alpine toadflax will do well in such a position, on gravel, as will most of the dwarf sedums or stone-crops, campanulas and the like. The great thing to aim at in the rock garden is the complete covering of the space with plant life, the only bare spots being a few actual rock projections.

Crazy Paving Crazy paving, which is one of the most satisfactory types of path for the rock garden, must be well and evenly laid, other-

13

Narcissus 'February Gold'

Flax (Linum)
Equally suitable for the rock
garden or fronts of borders

Dwarf daffodils (Narcissus)

15

wise it is very unpleasant to walk on, and will always be giving trouble because of the loosening and rising of the stones. The course of the path must be first marked out with stakes and the surface soil removed to the depth of from nine to twelve inches, if there is no lack of materials to fill it; the wider the path, the deeper the excavation necessary. The nature of the soil also affects the depth of excavation; in heavy clay at least twelve inches should be removed, in light soil nine inches will suffice.

There is a point that must be stressed here, and that is the importance of eradicating all perennial weeds, especially those with long, creeping roots, from the soil at the bottom and sides of the path. If this is not done, all kinds of weeds will soon make their appearance in the new path, and will be very difficult to get rid of. Weed-killer *will* kill these perennial weeds, but it takes three or four years to effect a thorough clearance. From one-third to one-half the depth excavated for the path must be filled up with rough stones, brickbats, clinkers from the brickfields, slag and scoriæ from the ironworks, or any coarse, hard rubbish that can be gathered together; the greater part of the remainder must then be filled up with coarse gravel, shingle, etc., which may be mixed with a little earth to give consistency to the whole. The correct level for the crown of the path can be marked by wooden pegs driven in to the right depth. Allow the path to set for a few days before using it.

The one great aim is to afford a sound and level surface for the paving, and the straight-edge will, therefore, be constantly in use with a view to this. The foundations must be rammed and rolled absolutely firm; if there is the slightest fear of any settlement in the base, as may well happen in clay, a two to three inch layer of cement in which to lay the paving had better be put down. Over the hard core spread a two-inch layer of sand or ashes, if cement is not used. Make this quite level and then lay down the paving, fitting the pieces carefully together and filling up the gaps with the smaller fragments. No crevices of much more than an inch in width should be left between the stones, or the path will not remain firm. Where there is likely to be much traffic, the main stones, and all those at the sides of the walk, should be set in mortar. This will keep it firm. Fill the interstices with sandy loam, so that rock plants, such as saxifrages, thymes, and other creepers and trailers, may be planted.

The selection of plants

The selection of plants for the rock garden gives rise to the very

16

vexed question of what are really suitable. Should only high alpines be included? Are all herbaceous perennials worthy inmates? What about the dwarf trees and shrubs? Are annuals allowable? Ask half a dozen rock-garden enthusiasts these questions, and you will get a different answer from each of them. As to herbaceous perennials and shrubs, height is a deciding factor, except in large rock gardens, where some of the taller of them will not come amiss in the more remote and out-of-the-way spots. Dwarf annuals, as a whole, would appear to be allowable as temporary subjects in new and sparsely-furnished gardens, while certain species are so charming and appropriate that they might well become permanencies. However, it is impossible to dogmatize on such a subject, and the final decision can quite well be left to the personal likes and dislikes of the owner of the rock garden. There are, however, several other points to be borne in mind. We should aim at having bloom over the longest possible period of the year. In this connection some of the smaller-growing bulbs, which bloom in the winter and early spring are invaluable, while those later autumn-flowering alpines, such as *Lithospermum diffusum*, syn. *prostratum* (Gromwell), *Erigeron mucronatus*, and *Zauschneria californica*, furnish colour long after the great majority of rock plants have finished flowering.

Some of the stronger growers soon overrun the rock garden and smother other plants less luxuriant, perhaps, but more beautiful and useful. These vigorous plants must, therefore, be limited in number and those of this nature that are chosen must be sternly cut back and kept in check. To add interest to the rock garden, as many of the various genera as possible should be selected, but the garden must never be overcrowded. Bulbs are often overlooked when planting the rock garden. This should not be, for few sights are more lovely than some of the smaller-growing bulbs blooming above a carpeting of *Acaena microphylla*, *Globularia nana*, *Arenaria balearica*, or other dwarf trailer.

In a newly-constructed garden there are sure to be some bare spaces for a year or so. Here it is that some of the dwarf annuals can be made to play such a useful part in filling the unavoidable gaps. The profusion and brightness of the bloom of most of these little plants, in addition to their value as fill-ups, justifies their position in the garden. A selection of suitable plants is given on pages 41–44.

Planting

Like all other plants, rock plants vary in their characteristics, habits, likes and dislikes. Some have a rounded growth, others are prostrate;

17

Pinks (*Dianthus alpinus*) is suitable for the rock garden.

Daisies (Bellis)
Shown here in a border but excellent for the rock garden

some love the sun, others the shade; a dry and sandy soil suits many when they can obtain a deep root run, others must have a moist, rich loam. In planting, therefore, the varying types should be grouped together according to habits and requirements, so that all shall have, as far as is possible, the conditions best for them.

It is always advisable to plant three or more specimens of a certain species or variety together, so as to form broad masses of colour rather than the patchwork effect caused by the indiscriminate planting of single subjects. The size of the groups naturally depends on the extent of the rock garden. In small gardens it may be wise to plant only single specimens.

There is yet another point to settle in this connection. It will be necessary to decide whether it is preferable to plant a comparatively limited number of fast-growing species that will spread rapidly over the bare spaces and quickly furnish the rock garden, or whether it is better to plant a greater number of plants, choicer in bloom, may be, but less rampant in habit. In the first case, a good show of bloom should be available in a year or so, but if the latter method is selected, patience will be needed for two or three years at least. The latter is the correct and better way, for the greater number of species planted will provide vastly more interest and pleasure. In any case, too many plants of the rampageous type should not be planted or they will soon choke the slower-growing specimens living among them.

Choice plants will need constant attention, or they are sure to be overwhelmed by their more vigorous neighbours.

Rock plants should be planted out either in the spring, or better still, in the late summer, but not later than September, since the roots make but little growth after that month, and the plants are liable to be washed out of the earth by heavy rain, or lifted from the soil by the action of frost. It is more usual to plant out alpines in the spring, particularly in or near our towns or cities, but, as already stated, it is better to do it in the summer, after they have bloomed, at which period their roots put forth new shoots and are more easily able to obtain a footing and to secure nourishment. If the plants are moved in spring, they are almost immediately subjected to the strain of flowering and get little support from their roots. This ought to be risked, however, in and around our larger cities, as many of the rarer alpines find a difficulty in withstanding the winter's fog and damp, even when well established. If care is taken, all alpines can be planted out at any time between early April and the end of August. They should be planted very firmly with the soil rammed well down around the roots, which should be carefully spread out; never should they be cramped. The plants must be thoroughly watered after planting, particularly in the spring. Specimens from pots may, of course, be planted at any time, provided a sufficient "ball" of soil from the pot is allowed to remain round the roots, and the weather is neither too dry nor too wet.

Do not plant out in very dry weather, as it will be extremely difficult to provide the roots with sufficient moisture; likewise, planting when very wet will make the soil become caked so hard that the fibrous roots will have difficulty in penetrating it and finding nourishment. After planting, especially in the case of the choicer alpines, small stone chippings should be spread over the surface of the soil around the plants. This will help to prevent excessive evaporation.

When planting in a crevice it is essential that there shall be no air-pocket at the bottom; this would drain all moisture from the roots and parch them. To avoid this, first ram plenty of good gritty soil deeply into the crevice and make sure that the bottom is well filled, then scrape out some of the mould at the top and set the plant in firmly, pressing the soil well down round the roots, and fix it in tightly by means of a smaller wedge of stone. Care should be taken that shade-lovers, like *Aquilegias* and *Anemones,* are given congenial situations; plants which prosper in the sun, as *Alyssums, Arabis, Zauschnerias,* etc., should be given the sunniest spots in the rock garden. Such plants as *Saxifrages* and *Aubrietas* should be planted in the crevices among the rocks; on the flat, lower-lying situations the larger *Primulas* and *Campanulas* will thrive; while an occasional dwarf evergreen shrub or conifer should certainly be planted.

Protection of plants in winter

Plants whose leaves are covered with fluff or down are, when in their natural haunts, usually protected from damp during the winter by a coat of snow. When they are grown out of doors in this country, they must, therefore, be given a covering of glass during the winter months; that is, from the middle of October to the beginning of March. When the plant is a small one nestling in a crevice between the rocks, it is often possible to cover it with a sheet of glass resting on the surrounding rocks; but when this cannot be done, four pieces of stiff galvanized wire should be inserted firmly in the ground and bent over at the top to hold the glass plate securely in position over the plant. If the weather is especially severe or the plant very delicate, four additional pieces of glass may be set in the soil and supported by the wires so as to form four walls protecting the plant. Sufficient space between the glass roof and the tops of the four walls should be left

Three varieties of irises
The dwarf species are excellent for the rock garden
and the tall species for the margins of pools

Grape hyacinth (Muscari)

for adequate ventilation (but not enough to admit the rain or snow) or the plants will be liable to damp-off. Hand-lights and bell-glasses may also be used, but in all cases adequate ventilation should be provided. The frost will often raise the plants from the soil, especially those planted the previous summer. In spring, therefore, each plant should be carefully scrutinized, and, if necessary, gently pressed down into the soil. Dead leaves must be removed from around the plants, and a top-dressing of fine chippings $\frac{1}{4}$ inch to dust with a little leaf-mould should be sifted round and close up to the crowns.

Care of the rock garden in spring, summer and autumn

All through the summer months the rock garden must be periodically weeded and all dead flower heads should be cut away. Water the choicer species during dry spells, even in spring if very dry, and in May top-dress with a thin layer of gritty loam and leaf-mould to which a little well-decayed cow-dung has been added. By July most of the plants will have borne the best of their bloom, and many of the most vigorous, such as *Arabis* and *Aubrieta* for example will now be pushing forth new growth, and will commence to overcrowd the less rampageous inmates of the rock garden. These plants, including the shrubby subjects, should, therefore, be trimmed back, and at the same time the older portions of the plants and all dead stems and foliage should be removed. Do not, however, cut the plants back so evenly that they have the symmetrical and formal aspect of shrubs in a topiary garden; rather endeavour to foster the wild and natural appearance of the rock garden, and where a plant is not throttling its neighbour and has ample space, let it ramble over the rocks at will. The soil should be well hoed up between the plants and any vacancies filled. At this time, too, divide the roots of plants that are to be increased and set the little plantlets in their new positions; likewise transplant any subjects that have not done well during the past season, and give them another chance in some other position and in different soil or with a different neighbour, for alpines, even of the same genera, will not always thrive when given identical conditions, but will have their likes and dislikes which arouse one's interest and study, and they often flourish when given a change.

In an old rock garden it may be that plants are not doing well because the soil in the pockets and crevices in which they grow is sour or exhausted. In such cases the plants should be removed and fresh soil, of a composition to suit the plants, should be inserted. This may be done in early spring or after flowering, the latter time being preferable as the plants have then a better chance of becoming established before the flowering season. If a plant has grown too large for the pocket it occupies, it should be lifted and divided: the stronger outer crowns only being replaced.

It should be remembered that established plants, if the rock garden has been properly constructed, will need watering only after a long spell of dry weather. If in such a case watering is necessary, let the plants have a good soaking in the evening once a week rather than a mere sprinkling every day; this latter process merely draws the roots to the surface and does more harm than good.

The propagation of rock plants

It is always advisable to have a few young plants coming on to replace casualties, for some alpines, especially the more interesting, have a habit of dying off suddenly.

Rock plants may be increased by seed sown under glass as soon as ripe or in March, by cuttings, or by division of roots in April or late Summer. It is better to raise alpines from cuttings or division or roots, rather than from seed, which is a lengthy and, in some cases, a difficult process.

The water garden

To be successful with a water garden, an adequate water supply must be assured, for aquatic plants will not survive being dried up for any length of time. While a stream gives the most natural setting for a water garden of the larger informal type, many streams dry up completely in a warm summer, and care must be taken that reliance is not placed on such a stream. Where only a small water capacity is involved, circulating it by means of a fractional h.p. electric pump is often cheaper than paying for replacement water, and the installation can usually be so arranged that, to all appearances, the supply is a constant one.

The best position for the water garden depends very largely on what form it takes. Where it consists solely of a formal pool, it is best to treat it as a main feature in its own right, and to place it in a conspicuous spot. It should not be under trees, as this not only detracts from its appeal as a centre-piece, but the water becomes fouled by the falling leaves, while water-lilies in the pool are deprived of much of the sunshine that they need. The tree-roots can also damage the structure of the pool. For the more informal pool, a low-lying piece of land should be chosen.

Phlox. There are several dwarf or alpine species

Water-lily tulips 'Johann Strauss'
Seen here with Chionodoxa (Glory of the Snow)

Dwarf tulips "Greigii" hybrid

Constructing a pool

The formal pool For most gardens the choice will be for the formal pool made of concrete, with or without a surround for the growing of marsh plants. Having the pool at ground level saves considerable expense, though it does make it more dangerous for young children, and precautions will have to be taken to prevent them falling in. To construct it the shape should be marked out on the ground, and the soil excavated to the required depth, from eighteen inches to three feet according to the size of the pool, plus the thickness of the concrete base. Where there is to be a surround for an aquatic border this should be included in the excavated areas, as this border will be inside the pool structure. When the excavation is complete, all loose soil must be shovelled out and the bottom made thoroughly firm. The weight of the concrete and the water is considerable, and if the base is not really firm there is a danger of the concrete cracking. Before any concreting is done, the pipes for supplying the water and for draining the pool must be put in position, and there should be an overflow pipe. The local plumber will give advice on this. The concrete should be made of four parts of aggregate not larger than $\frac{3}{4}$ inch, two parts sand and one part cement. A six-inch layer of this concrete should be placed over the bottom of the excavated area and should be "worked" with a shovel to ensure that no air-spaces or "voids" are left in it, after which it

A formal pool in a patio

should be firmed and levelled, but not made too smooth or the cement lining which is to be applied later, will not grip. Next erect a layer of temporary boards four inches from the vertical sides, so that with the soil it forms a mould into which the concrete to form the sides A and A′ will be poured. If possible this side concrete should be put in position while the base concrete is still wet and unset, as the two will then bind together and there will be no joint in the construction. To achieve this the boarding should be prefabricated, so that it can be dropped into position without delay. When the concrete has well set, the pool should be made completely watertight by lining it with a cement, consisting of one part of cement to three of sand, plus a waterproofing material in the recommended proportion. This should be applied from $\frac{1}{2}$ to one inch thick, and is best put on in two coats, giving the second coat while the first is still fresh but firm. Care should be taken to see that the corners EE are completely watertight. Where a surround for plants is to be included, the inner walls C and C′ can be constructed after the concrete has set. They should be from twelve inches to thirty inches from the edge of the pool proper, in proportion to its size, and from eight inches to ten inches lower than the sides. Apertures must be left in the bottom of the wall to allow for the passage of water, when the pool is emptied. When the concrete is thoroughly dry, the spaces M and M′ between the retaining walls A and C and A′ and C′ are filled with a compost of loam and peat, or loam and leaf-mould. The soil may then be banked up so that the tops of the walls A and A′ are covered with soil and hidden from sight.

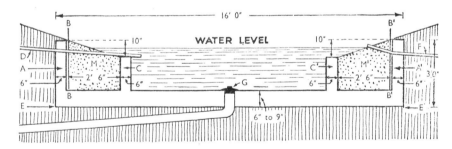

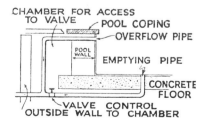

A system with controlled emptying pipe combined with an overflow. It is cheap and easy to install

Plantain Lily (Hosta)
Attractive plants for the margins of water gardens

A formal water garden
featuring water lilies.
A layout of this type
can be scaled down to
suit the small garden.

Weeping willow (Salix)

The bog or marsh gardens

The informal pool For larger and less formal gardens, a pool to match these conditions will be needed. Its actual shape will of course depend on the contours of the land, and of the general landscaping of the area in which it is to be situated. Its design should in all cases be simple. Curves and water are complementary and the beauty of one is appreciably lessened by the absence of the other, but the curves must be sweeping and graceful and they must flow as naturally as does the water which they bound. And the softness and serenity of the scene is much enhanced if grass grows down the sloping banks to the water's edge, and further interest is added to the scene if marsh-loving plants are planted along limited stretches of the banks. These larger pools or ponds are seldom concreted as the thickness needed to ensure freedom from cracking over the comparatively large area would make the cost prohibitive. The most practicable method for these pools is "puddling", but this needs a nine-inch layer of clay which must either be present as sub-soil, or must be easily available from elsewhere. This puddling consists of pummelling the moist clay with a rammer, until it takes on the consistency of dough and is impermeable to water, after which it must not be allowed to become at all dry, or serious cracking will take place.

Plastic pools Prefabricated pools of various shapes are now available and are perfectly satisfactory for use on a small scale. The soil should be excavated to make a good fit, particularly along the bottom so that there are no spaces where, in time, stretching may occur. For more informal pools plastic sheeting may be used and here again the excavation must be neatly finished off so that the sheeting will lie closely along the bottom and the sides which should be gently sloping. In both cases the edges of the pools may be concealed with rocks or paving which, with a sheeted pool, must be heavy enough to hold the edges in position.

The bog or marsh garden

A pond is not an essential part of the bog garden, although if there is one its overflow can be used to feed the marsh. What is important, however, is that the soil of the marsh garden be kept in a moist, swampy state throughout the whole year. The site of the bog garden must be low-lying and where the surface drainage will collect naturally. If the sub-soil is of sticky clay, a mere trickle of water will keep the ground in a sufficiently moist condition. Should the sub-soil be light and well drained, a certain amount of excavation will be necessary before the bog garden can be made.

32

Dig out about two feet of the top soil and introduce a little clay to form a basis, over this spread a five-inch bed of rubble or large stones, and then a layer of coarse soil. Now fill the hollow, almost to the level of the surrounding land, with a compost of half loam and half leaf-mould or peat. Unless a natural flow of water is available, an artificial trickle, just sufficient to keep the bog swampy, must be introduced. Because bog plants should never suffer from drought, the marsh garden should be kept quite moist, but on the other hand must not become stagnant, and it is for this reason that slight bottom drainage is introduced. The bog should never be more than two feet in depth; its extent, of course, will depend on the space available and upon individual need.

Paths of rough stones or bricks should be made through the bog, and over these should be placed flat stepping-stones, so that one can get to every part of the bog. If these paths are made at varying heights, they may be used to divide the bog into shelving beds, the higher and better-drained of which will accommodate plants not requiring over-much moisture, while in the lower-lying sites can be grown the real moisture-lovers.

Almost any moisture-loving plant may be grown, as can all the subjects that are usually to be found at the margins of streams and ponds, even some of those which at times have six inches or more of water over their crowns. All plants growing freely in shallow water may also be grown in the bog garden. Be careful not to overcrowd plants, rather group together three to five plants of the same kind, leave a space, and again plant a clump of subjects of different colour, type and height. This irregularity and variety will please the eye, which would otherwise tend to become overdone by a mass of the same colour, size and form.

The actual marsh plants selected will, of course, depend upon the layout and size of the garden; the natural surroundings must also be very carefully considered. If the area is restricted, greater variety and beauty can be obtained by the use of dwarf-growing species, while among extensive surroundings full rein may be given to the freer-growing plants, many of which are invaluable as a background where space permits. It is always necessary, however, to bear in mind the size to which the plants will grow in from two to three years, and to arrange them accordingly. The most usual fault is overcrowding, and it is wise to avoid this at any cost. Also, study the plants in their native haunts, and then, when planting them, endeavour to give them as natural a site as possible.

Several varieties of
water lilies (Nymphaea)

The moraine or scree garden

Many rare and more fastidious plants must have conditions more exactly like those in which they grow naturally. They grow on mountain slopes covered with loose stones, where the melting snow in summer provides them with plenty of ice-cold water and a blanket of snow protects them in winter.

Conditions of adequate moisture and good drainage, and protection from damp in winter, are achieved with the help of moraine. This can be made quite cheaply anywhere in the rock garden. Plants requiring very diverse kinds of soil may thus grow in close proximity to one another.

To construct the moraine, dig a basin about two-and-a-half feet deep. Make it slope slightly towards the front, but not too steeply or the moraine will become over-dry in summer. Make the lower ten inches of the basin watertight with cement or by puddling it with clay. Construct an outlet in front which will hold about ten inches of water when closed. When the outlet is open no water should remain in the basin. Cover the bottom of the trench with about six inches of rubble, stones or any material that will afford good drainage. Above this place another six inches or so of stones roughly one inch in diameter. These will prevent the grit sinking through and blocking the drainage, and will also assist the capillary action to lift the moisture on the warmer days.

Fill up the hollow with a mixture of stone chips and gravel. Cover this with a layer one inch thick, formed from a mixture of equal parts of ordinary garden soil, peat and small stone chips, preferably limestone or sandstone chips. Place a few boulders in the moraine to break up the surface and give the plants more protection. Make sure you give sufficient moisture each day to cause an overflow from the outlet at the bottom of the moraine. You can do this by leading a natural trickle of water into the top of the moraine or by daily watering from a can. The outlet should be left open from November to May, when no additional moisture is needed in the moraine.

You can also lead the overflow into a pool, thus adding to the garden's attractions. It may contain rushes and small water plants, and its overflow in turn will provide an excellent situation for bog plants or for alpines which love much moisture.

Many plants that have proved failures in the rock garden will flourish in the moraine. Moraine inhabitants are not so rampant as many alpines in the rock garden proper. Nevertheless, the more vigorous ones should be kept in check. A light top dressing of loam and peat, with an equal part of stone chips ($\frac{1}{4}$ to $\frac{3}{8}$ inch), is required in spring and early autumn.

An ideal position for the moraine is in the sun on the slope of a miniature valley between two rocky spurs, with the gorge gradually spreading into a flat bed of scree, strewn with occasional boulders. If the garden is large the moraine may cover an area of many square yards. On the other hand, it may be no more than a small, well-drained pocket or crevice filled with moraine mixture in which only a single specimen can grow.

Dry walls

Dry walls, with suitable plants in the crevices between the stones and trailing down the face of the walls, have become increasingly popular. They are usually retaining walls; often only one side of them is exposed, the other side being laid against the vertical or near-vertical surface between two different levels of land.

The best time to construct a dry wall is in March or April, because it is best to plant the walls as construction proceeds, and at this time root action is most vigorous. Plants to go in the wall should have their roots thoroughly moistened before lifting, and the roots should be well spread out in the soil between the stones forming the wall, keeping them central so that they have a good layer of soil both above and below them. This will enable them to get established quickly in the soil in the wall, after which the roots will penetrate into the soil behind, and that will then form their main source of sustenance. The best position for a plant is near the base of a vertical "joint", where it is likely to keep more moist than higher up in the joint.

As no mortar is used in the construction of the dry wall, the space between the stones has to be filled with earth, and as this earth will in the early stages have to support the plants, it must be of fairly open texture and have an adequate amount of nutrient in it. It must not have a large amount of bulky manure in it, however, or this will quickly decompose and so leave gaps in the soil which will loosen the whole structure of the wall. A better mixture is of medium texture loam, lightened if necessary by the addition of coarse sand, with four ounces of either bone meal or John Innes base fertilizer added to every bushel and thoroughly mixed in. The amount of soil needed will be approximately a quarter of the total space that the wall will occupy.

The dry wall is usually made of natural stones, either sandstone or limestone, roughly rectangular, between two inches and eight inches in thickness, and with a minimum width of six inches. The less they are trimmed the more natural will the wall appear. The first thing to

Milfoil (Achillea)
The species A. umbellata
is best for the dry wall

Wallflower (Cheiranthus)
The dwarf varieties
are excellent for the
dry wall and rock garden

Tickseed (Coreopsis) growing on a dry wall

do is to prepare the soil face which will provide the backing for the wall. Where it will be two-and-a-half feet or less high it can be vertical, but for higher walls a slope of one in six is advisable. The next thing is to ensure that there is a firm foundation for the wall, by taking out a trench about six inches deep and slightly wider than the stones which will form the base of the wall. There is no need to put in a concrete foundation, but the soil should be well rammed to give a solid base, but sloping slightly towards the back so that the stones are slightly tilted in that direction. On this sound footing place the first layer of stones, using the largest available, and keeping their upper surfaces at one horizontal level, making adjustments with the soil underneath to achieve this. If the stones are of moderate size, the vertical gaps between them should be about three inches wide, but with smaller stones, proportionately smaller gaps should be left. The horizontal gaps should be about one inch wide. These gaps should be firmly packed with the prepared soil and care must be taken to see that any crevices between the back of the wall and the vertical soil face are also filled in and firmed. Any air-pockets left there will not only weaken the wall structurally, but will cause rapid drying out of the plants' root systems.

Care must be taken in the planting, for while good solid "joints" must be made, the plants obviously cannot be rammed too hard. With a little practice it is soon possible to achieve a happy mean which meets both needs. When the first layer or "course" has been completed, succeeding courses should be added, but the stones should be bonded, so that any vertical crevice will be as near as possible to the centre of the stone below it. Unless this is done a wall will very quickly collapse. The top of the wall is best left flat, so that the rain may soak in, but a six-inch layer of soil should be made firm on the top and in this, at intervals, large stones can be placed. These will help to keep the soil in place and will supply a moist root-run for plants like rock-roses and saxifrages which can be planted there. It is possible to plant the wall itself after it has been constructed, but generally it is not so satisfactory as planting as construction proceeds. A list of plants suitable for a dry wall is given in the table at the end of this work.

SELECTIVE LIST OF PLANTS FOR THE ROCK GARDEN

SPECIES	COMMON NAME	HT. INS.	FLOWER PERIOD	COLOUR OF FLOWERS
Acaena buchananii	New Zealand Burr	5–7	Summer	Bright red
microphylla		2	Summer	Crimson
Acantholimon glumaceum	Prickly Thrift	5–7	Summer	Rose or pale pink
Achillea ageratifolia	Milfoil, Yarrow	2–4	Summer	White
tomentosa		9	Summer	Yellow
Adonis vernalis	Pheasant's Eye	12	Apr.	Yellow or white
Acthionema 'Warley Rose'		9	May–June	Deep pink
Alchemilla vulgaris	Lady's Mantle	6	June–Aug.	Yellowish-green
Alyssum saxatile	Madwort	12	Apr.–June	Rich yellow
Androsace carnea	Rock Jasmine	3	Spring	White
foliosa		6	Summer	Pink and yellow
sarmentosa		4	May	Rose
Anemone apennina	Windflower	6	Mar.–Apr.	White, rose, blue
blanda		6	Mar.	White, blue
nemorosa		6	Mar.	Various
Anthyllis montana		2–4	June	Pink, rose
Antirrhinum asarina	Snapdragon	6	Summer	Yellow
Aquilegia glandulosa	Columbine	8–12	May–June	Blue
Arabis albida	Rock Cress	6–9	Apr.–Mar.	White or pink
alpina		6	Apr.–Mar.	White
Armeria maritima	Thrift, Sea Pink, etc.	6–12	June–July	White or pink
Asperula nitida	Woodruff	4–6	July–Aug.	Rose
Aster alpinus		6–9	July	Red or purple
Astilbe simplicifolia	Goat's Beard	6–7	June–July	White or pink
Bellis perennis	Daisy	6–10	May–June	White, pink, red
Bellium minutum		3	Summer	Whitish
Bulbocodium vernum	Spring Meadow Saffron	4–6	Jan.–Mar.	Purple-red
Calandrinia umbellata	Rock Purslane	6–9	Summer	Bright crimson
Cerastium tomentosum	Snow-in-Summer	6	June–Aug.	White
Cheiranthus cheiri (dwarf vars.)	Wallflower	6–9	Apr.–June	Various
Cotula dioica		2–4	Summer	Yellow

SPECIES	COMMON NAME	HT. INS.	FLOWER PERIOD	COLOUR OF FLOWERS
Cyclamen europaeum	Sowbread	2–4	Autumn	White, rose, carmine
Dianthus alpinus	Pink	4	June	White, pink or reddish
Draba aizoon		6	Spring	Bright yellow
rigida		3	Spring	Golden yellow
Dryas octopetala	Mountain Avens	3	June–July	White
Epimedium alpinum		6–9	June	Red and yellow
Erigeron foliosus-confinis	Flea Bane	12	July–Aug.	Mauve
Erinus alpinus	Sum. Starwort	2–3	Apr.–June	White, purple
Erodium absinthoides	Heron's Bill	6	July	Pink, white, violet
macradeum		4	June–July	Violet-pink
Erysimum alpinum	Fairy Wallflower	6	May	Sulphur
Erythronium dens-canis	Dog's Tooth Violet	6	Mar.–Apr.	White or purplish
Frankenia laevis		4–6	July	Pinkish
Fritillaria acmopetala		12–18	Spring	Green and purplish-brown
caucasica		8–12	Spring	Purplish-brown and greenish-blue
Galanthus nivalis	Snowdrop	6	Jan.–Feb.	White
Gentiana acaulis		2–4	May–June	Deep blue
farreri		8–10	July–Aug.	Blue, tinged red
sino-ornata		4–6	Sept.–Oct.	Dark blue
Geranium aconitifolium	Crane's Bill	9–18	May–June	White
cinereum		6	June	Purplish-pink
Geum heldreichii	Avens	9–12	June–Oct.	Orange-red
montanum		6–12	June–July	Yellow or orange
Globularia cordifolia	Globe Daisy	3–4	Summer	White, rose, blue
Gypsophila repens		4–6	June–Aug.	White, rose
Haberlea rhodopensis		6	May	White, pale lilac
Houstonia caerulea	Bluets	3–6	Summer	White, blue
Hutchinsia alpina		2–4	May–June	White
Hypericum polyphyllum	St. John's Wort	9–12	July–Sept.	Golden yellow
Iberis sempervirens	Candytuft	6–12	May–June	White
Iris histrio		6–10	Jan.	Lilac
Jasione jankae	Sheep's Scabious	6	Summer	Blue
montana		9	Summer	Pale blue or white
Leontopodium alpinum	Edelweiss	4–6	June–July	Pale cream
Lewisia cotyledon		8–10	Apr.–May	White
Linaria alpina	Toadflax	4	Summer	White, pink or violet
Linum alpinum	Flax	6	July–Aug.	Pale blue

42

SPECIES	COMMON NAME	HT. INS.	FLOWER PERIOD	COLOUR OF FLOWERS
Lithospermum diffusum	Gromwell	12	Summer	Deep blue
Meconopsis quintuplinervia		12	May–Aug.	Lilac-blue
villosa		18	May–Aug.	Yellow
Mentzelia lindleyi		12–15	June–Oct.	Golden yellow
Mertensia primuloides		4–6	May–Aug.	Deep blue
Morisia monantha	Mediterranean Cress	2–3	Mar.–May	Golden yellow
Muscari botryoides	Grape Hyacinth	8–12	Spring	Deep or pale blue
moschatum	Musk Hyacinth	8–10	Spring	Yellow or purple
Nierembergia caerulea	Bell Flower	6–12	Summer	Bluish-violet
repens		3–6	June–July	Creamy white
Omphalodes linifolia	Venus' Navel-wort	6–12	June–Aug.	White
verna	Blue-eyed Mary	2–6	Apr.–May	Light blue
Ononis cenisia		3–9	June–Aug.	Purplish-pink
Onosma echiodies		6–8	Summer	White or pale yellow
stellulatum		2–4	Summer	Yellow
Origanum dictamus	Dittany	8–12	Summer	Pink
Ourisia alpina		4–10	Summer	Red or pink
coccinea		6–12	Summer	Scarlet
Oxalis enneaphylla		6–8	Summer	White or pink
Pelargonium endlicherianum		8–12	Early Summer	Pink
Penstemon cobaea	Beard Tongue	12	June–Aug.	White or purple
newberryi		6	Summer	Pink or cerise
Phlox subulata		3–9	Apr.–May	White, pink, blue
Phyteuma comosum	Horned Rampion	3–6	July	Purplish-blue
Polemonium reptans	Jacob's Ladder	6–18	Apr.–May	White or blue
Polygonum affine	Knotweed	9–12	Aug.–Oct.	Red
Potentilla nitida	Cinquefoil	6	May–Aug.	White or pink
Primula auricula		6–9	Apr.–May	Various
Puschkinia scilloides	Striped Squill	4–6	Apr.–May	Blue to whitish
Pyrola minor	Wintergreen	1–3	June–July	Pinky-white
rotundifolia		6–8	June–Aug.	White
Ramonda myconi		6	May–Aug.	White, rose or purple
Sagina glabra	Pearlwort	1–4	Summer	White
Sanguinaria canadensis	Bloodroot	4–6	Apr.–May	White
Saponaria ocymoides	Soapwort	6	May–June	White, pink or rose
Saxifraga spp.		9–18	May–July	Various

SPECIES	COMMON NAME	HT. INS.	FLOWER PERIOD	COLOUR OF FLOWERS
Scabiosa graminifolia		9	July	Rose or mauve
Scilla hispanica	Spanish Squill	6–9	Apr.–May	White, pink or blue
sibirica		4–6	Mar.	Blue or white
Sedum acre	Stonecrop	2–3	May–June	Yellow
spathulifolium		3	June–July	Yellow
Sempervivum arachnoideum	Houseleek	4–6	June–July	Reddish-pink
montanum		4–6	June–Aug.	White or purplish-white
Sibthorpia europaea	Cornish Money-wort	2	July	Pink and yellow
Silene acaulis	Moss Campion	2	May–June	White, pink or rose
rupestris		4–6	June–Aug.	White or pink
Soldanella alpina		4–6	Apr.–May	Violet-blue
Symphyandra wanneri		6	Summer	Blue
Teucrium chamaedrys		6–18	July–Sept.	Rose
Thalictrum alpinum	Meadow Rue	4–6	July–Aug.	Purplish
Townsendia grandiflora		8–12	Summer	Blue or violet
Trientalis borealis		6–9	Apr.–May	White
Tunica saxifraga		4–8	June–Sept.	White or lilac
Veronica cineraria	Speedwell	6	May–Sept.	Pink
nummularia		2–4	May–Sept.	Blue or pink
Wahlenbergia hederacea		4–8	Summer	Pale blue
Wulfenia carinthiaea		12–14	June–Aug.	Purple-blue
Zauschneria californica		12–18	July–Sept.	Scarlet

SELECTIVE LIST OF PLANTS FOR THE WATER AND BOG GARDEN

SPECIES	COMMON NAME	HT. INS.	FLOWER PERIOD	COLOUR OF FLOWERS
Acorus calamus	Sweet Flag	30	July–Aug.	Yellow
gramineus		10	July–Aug.	Yellow
Alisma plantago-aquatica	Great Water Plantain	24–36	June–Aug.	Pale rose
Anagallis tenella	Bog Pimpernel	3	July	Pink
Aponogeton distachyus	Cape Pond-weed	4	Apr.–Oct.	White or rose
krauseanus		4	Apr.–Oct.	Cream or yellowish
Arundo donax	Great Weed	Up to 144		
Astilbe spp.	Goat's Beard	12–36	June–Aug.	White, pink or red
Butomus umbellatus	Flowering Rush	30	June–Aug.	Rose

SPECIES	COMMON NAME	HT. INS.	FLOWER PERIOD	COLOUR OF FLOWERS
Calla palustris	Bog Arum	6	June–Aug.	White
Caltha palustris	Marsh Marigold	12	May–July	Rich yellow
Cardamine pratensis	Cuckoo Flower	12–18	Apr.–May	White or pale purple
Ceratophyllum demersum	Water Hornwort	—	—	—
Dodecantheon meadia	American Cow-slip	18–24	May	White or rose
Elodea crispa		—	—	—
Filipendula ulmaria	Meadow Sweet	24–48	June–Aug.	White
Fritillaria meleagris	Snake's Head	9–12	Spring	Purple, chequered white
Gentiana ascelepiadea		12–18	July–Aug.	Violet-blue
pneumonanthe		6–12	May–June	Deep-blue
Geum rivale	Avens	9–12	May–June	Pink or reddish
Gunnera chilensis		36–72	Summer	Reddish
manicata		Up to 8 ft.	Summer	Reddish
Hemerocallis (hybrids)	Day Lily			
Heracleum mantegazzianum	Cartwheel Flower	Up to 12 ft.	Summer	White
Hosta undulata	Plantain Lily	30	Aug.	Pale lilac
Hottonia palustris	Water violet	12–24	June	Lilac with yellow eye
Iris kaempheri		24–30	July	Various
pseudacorus	Yellow Flag	36–48	May–June	Yellow
sibirica		24–36	May–June	White, blue, purple
Ligularia clivorum		36–48	July–Aug.	Orange
Linnaea borealis	Twin-flower	2–4	June–July	White
Lysimachia clethroides		18–36	July–Sept.	White
nummularia	Creeping Jenny	Creep-ing	July–Aug.	Yellow
Lythrum salicaria	Purple Loose-strife	24–48	June–Sept.	Pink, red or purple
Menyanthes trifoliata	Marsh Trefoil	12	Mar.–June	Pinkish-white
Miscanthes sinensis	Eulalia	36	Aug.–Sept.	White tinged red
Myosotis scorpioides	Forget-me-not	6–12	May–Sept.	White or sky-blue
Nuphar advena	Yellow Water Lily	—	June–Sept.	Yellow
lutea		—	June–Sept.	Yellow
Nymphaea alba	Water Lily	—	June–Aug.	Various
marliaca		—	June–Aug.	Various
odorata		—	June–Aug.	Pink, white, yellow

SPECIES	COMMON NAME	HT. INS.	FLOWER PERIOD	COLOUR OF FLOWERS
Parnassia palustris	Grass of Parnassus	4–6	June–July	White
Peltandra virginica		24–36	June–July	White
Peltiphyllum peltatum	Umbrella Plant	36–48	Spring	White or pink
Phormium colensoi	New Zealand Flax	48–72	Summer	Yellowish
tenax		Up to 15 ft.	Summer	Dull red
Pinguicula grandiflora	Butterwort	4–6	Summer	Violet
Podophyllum emodi	May Apple	12	Apr.–May	White or rose
peltatum		12–24	Apr.–May	White
Pontederia cordata	Water Plantain	—	Summer	White or blue
Primula spp.	Primrose	4–12	May	Various
Ranunculus aconitifolius	Bachelor's Buttons	Up to 24	May–June	White
lingua		24–36	July–Sept.	Yellow
Sagittaria latifolia		12–36	Summer	White
sagittifolia	Common Arrowhead	12–18	Summer	White
Scirpus lacustris	Bulrush	Up to 8 ft.		
Stratiotes aloides	Water Soldier	—	Summer	White
Thalictrum flavum	Meadow Rue	24–36	July–Aug.	Yellow
Trillium erectum	Birth Root	12	May–June	Deep purple
grandiflorum	Wake Robin	12–18	Apr.–June	Rose
Trollius × cultorum	Globe Flower	24–36	May–July	Yellow to orange
Typha angustifolia	Small Reed Mace	36–48	July	Brown
latifolia	Reed Mace	Up to 8 ft.	July–Aug.	Dark brown
Xerophyllum asphodeloides		24–48	Summer	Ivory-white

SELECTIVE LIST OF PLANTS FOR THE DRY WALL

SPECIES	COMMON NAME	HT. INS.	FLOWER PERIOD	COLOUR OF FLOWERS
Acaena buchananii	New Zealand Burr	5–7	June–Aug.	Bright red
Acantholimon venustum	Prickly Thrift	6–8	July–Aug.	Rose or pale pink

SPECIES	COMMON NAME	HT. INS.	FLOWER PERIOD	COLOUR OF FLOWERS
Achillea tomentosa	Milfoil, Yarrow	6	July–Sept.	Yellow
Aethionema grandiflorum	Burnt Candytuft	12	May–July	Rose
Alyssum maritimum	Sweet Alyssum	4–6	May–July	White or lilac
saxatile		12	Apr.–June	Rich yellow
Androsace carnea	Rock Jasmine	3	Spring	White or rose
Antirrhinum	(Consult catalogues)			
Aquilegia alpina	Columbine	18	May–June	White and blue or blue
Arabis albida	Rock Cress	6–9	Apr.–Mar.	White or pink
androsacea		2	June–July	White
Arenaria balearica	Sandwort	3	Mar.–Aug.	White
Asperula nitida	Woodruff	4–6	July–Aug.	Rose
Aubrieta deltoidea		4	Apr.–June	Wide range
Bergenia purpurascens	Megasea	3–9	June	Purple
Campanula carpatica	Bellflower	12	June–Aug.	Blue
Cerastium tomentosum	Mouse Ear	6	June–Aug.	White
Cheiranthus cheiri	Wallflower	6–9	Apr.–June	Wide range
Corydalis lutea	Fumitory	12	May–June	Yellow
Dianthus alpinus	Pink	4	June	White, pink, purplish to red
deltoides	The Maiden Pink	9	June–Sept.	White, pink, purplish to red
Draba aizoon		6	Spring	Bright yellow
Dryas octopetala	Mountain Avens	3	June–July	White
Erigeron compositus	Flea Bane	6	June	White or pale blue
Erinus alpinus	Summer Star-wort	2–3	Apr.–June	White, purple or carmine
Erodium macradeum	Heron's Bill	4	June–July	Violet-pink
petraeum		4–6	June	Purple, violet or rose
Frittillaria caucasica		8–12	Spring	Purplish-brown
Gentiana × macaulayi		9–12	Sept.–Oct.	Deep blue
Gypsophila repens		4–6	June–Aug.	White or rose
Helichrysum orientale	Everlasting Flowers	6–18	Summer	Yellow
Iberis sempervirens	Candytuft	6–12	May–June	White
Kentranthus ruber	Valerian	24–36	June–July	White, pink or red
Leontopodium alpinum	Edelweiss	4–6	June–July	Cream
Linaria alpina	Toadflax	4	July–Sept.	White, pink or bluish-violet
Linum alpinum	Flax	6	July–Aug.	Pale blue
Mertensia alpina		8–12	May–Aug.	Light blue

SPECIES	COMMON NAME	HT. INS.	FLOWER PERIOD	COLOUR OF FLOWERS
Morisia monantha	Mediterranean Cress	2–3	Mar.–May	Golden yellow
Nepeta × faassenii	Catmint	12–18	May–Sept.	Pale lavender
Oenothera caespitosa	Evening Prim-rose	9–12	May–Aug.	White to pink
Onosma alba-pilosum		6–8	Summer	White changing to rose
Origanum hybridum		8–12	Summer	Pink
Phlox subulata		4–9	May–July	Wide range
Primula auricula	Auricula	6–9	Apr.–May	Wide range
Ramonda nathalie		6	May–Aug.	White or lavender
Saponaria ocymoides	Soapwort	6	May–June	White, pink or deep rose
Saxifraga				
Sedum spathalitolium	Stonecrop	3	June–July	Yellow
Sempervivum montanum		4–6	June– Aug.	White or purplish-violet
Thalictrum alpinum	Meadow Rue	4–6	July–Aug.	Purplish
Valeriana arizonica		3–4	Apr.–July	Pink
Wahlenbergia albomarginata		4–8	June	White or blue
Zauschneria californica		12–18	July–Sept.	Scarlet